THIS BOOK
BELONGS TO

Hinojosa

TELL ME
ABOUT THE BIBLE

By MARY ALICE JONES

Illustrated by PELAGIE DOANE

RAND McNALLY & COMPANY

NEW YORK   CHICAGO   SAN FRANCISCO

Library of Congress Catalog Card Number: 45-10489

CONTENTS

GOD'S BOOK

READ ME in the Bible," Bobby asked his mother.

His mother opened the Bible. "I know what I shall read you, Bobby. I shall read you a great poem about the beginning of the world."

"Show it to me in the Bible," Bobby said.

His mother showed him. "It is here, in the first pages of the Bible."

Bobby looked at the pages. "Why aren't there any pictures?"

"There are pictures in some copies of the Bible," his mother explained. "But don't you think it is good sometimes to make our own pictures in our minds?"

Bobby nodded his head. And his mother went on, "As I read to you, try to see pictures of the things the Bible story tells about."

"What does it tell about?" Bobby asked.

"About the very beginning. Before there were families or animals or flowers or the sun or moon or stars. Even before there was any earth or any sky or any light. It is about the very beginning when there was only God. God was planning the world. And the world came to be."

"I will close my eyes and listen," Bobby said. "Now I am all ready, Mother."

And so his mother read to him from the Bible. This is what she read:

IN THE beginning God created the heaven and the earth.

And the earth was without form and void, and darkness was upon the face of the deep.

And the spirit of God moved upon the face of the waters.

And God said, "Let there be light." And there was light.

And God saw the light that it was good; and God divided the light from the darkness.

And God called the light Day, and the darkness he called Night.

And the evening and the morning were the first day.

And God said, "Let there be a firmament in the midst of the waters, and let it divide the waters from the waters."

And God called the firmament Heaven.

And the evening and the morning were the second day.

And God said, "Let the waters under the heaven be gathered together unto one place, and let the dry land appear."

And God called the dry land Earth; and the gathering together of the waters called he Seas.

And God said, "Let the earth bring forth grass, the herb yielding seed, and the fruit tree yielding fruit."

And the evening and the morning were the third day.

And God said, "Let there be lights in the firmament of the heaven to divide the day from the night."

And God made two great lights: the greater light to rule the day, and the lesser light to rule the night; he made the stars also.

And the evening and the morning were the fourth day.

And God said, "Let the waters bring forth abundantly the moving creature that hath life, and fowl that may fly above the earth."

And the evening and the morning were the fifth day.

And God said, "Let the earth bring forth the living creature, cattle, and creeping thing, and beast of the earth."

And God said, "Let us make man in our image, after our likeness: and let them have dominion over the fish of the sea, and over the fowl of the air, and over the cattle, and over all the earth, and over every creeping thing."

So God created man in his own image, in the image of God created he him; male and female created he them.

And God blessed them.

And God saw everything that he had made, and, behold, it was very good.

And the evening and the morning were the sixth day.

And on the seventh day God rested from all his work which he had made.

And God blessed the seventh day, and sanctified it: because that in it he had rested from all his work which God had created and made.

From Genesis 1:1–31; 2:1–3

Bobby's mother closed the Bible. "Did you see the pictures, son?"

"In my mind I saw them," Bobby answered. "I saw the sun and the stars and the grass and the animals."

"I saw them, too," his mother said.

"Did God write that poem? Is it God's poem?" Bobby wanted to know.

"It really is God's poem, dear. God thought of it. But God did not write it with a pencil or a typewriter, the way Daddy writes his letters."

"Then how did he write it?"

"This is the way I think it was," his mother explained. "After

[11]

men had begun to live on the earth, some of them wondered about the world. They wondered how the world had been made. They wondered how men had been made. They wondered and wondered."

"Then did God tell them?" Bobby asked.

"It took men a long time to understand, son. God showed them all the beauty of the earth. He showed them food to eat and water to drink which he had planned."

"I should think *somebody* would know God made it," Bobby said.

"Some men did come to know, Bobby. Because they listened, God spoke to them. They knew that God planned the world. They began to understand that God made man to be God's helper. By and by there was a wise man and a good man who was a poet, too.

"This man thought, 'God has helped me to understand about the world. He has helped me to understand why he made man. But many men do not understand. They do not even know that God planned the world. God wants them to know. He wants me to tell them. I will write down what God has shown me'."

Bobby thought awhile. "I like the poem," he said. "It is a big poem. Read it to me again."

So Bobby's mother read it to him again.

BIBLE STORYTELLERS

BOBBY and his little sister Mary and their mother were riding on the train. They were going to visit Grandmother. Mary was taking a nap, curled up on one seat. Bobby and his mother were sitting on the other. Bobby's mother had been telling him a story.

"I like to listen to stories, riding along on the train," Bobby said.

His mother laughed. "Is that the only time you like to listen to stories?" she asked.

Bobby laughed, too. His mother and his daddy and his teacher and his grandmother and everybody who knew Bobby knew how he liked stories. "I think I like to hear stories almost all the time,"

he said. "But Susan and John and Henry like them, too. Don't all children like stories?"

"Almost all children do," his mother agreed. "And most grown-ups do, too."

Bobby was pleased. "Do they, Mother? Do you like stories?"

"Ever so much, son. People have always liked stories. Long, long ago before there were any books there were storytellers."

"Tell me about it," Bobby said. "About the storytellers before there were any books."

His mother thought a moment. "The storytellers of long ago were important persons, Bobby," she said. "The people depended upon them. They trusted them. Sometimes the storytellers told made-up stories. But more often they told real stories about their own people. They told stories about heroes, about strong men and good men."

"Tell me some more," Bobby asked.

"The storytellers of long ago helped to give us our Bible, Bobby."

Bobby looked surprised. "How could they, Mother? The Bible is God's book."

"Yes, it is, Bobby, but God often lets persons help him. And the storytellers helped him give us the Bible."

"What did they do?"

"The storytellers traveled about more than the other people. They learned more about what had happened. They heard about the great men. And so they knew more than the other people.

"Often they were alone and they wondered about all they had heard and seen. And often they thought of God. God helped them to understand about the world. God helped them to understand how he wanted men to live."

"And did they tell the people?" Bobby asked.

His mother nodded her head. "When they traveled about from place to place, they told the people what they had learned. They told them how God helped men to be great and good."

"But how did all these stories get in our Bible, Mother?" Bobby wanted to know.

"It was long, long after the stories were told, Bobby. But because the storytellers had told the stories so well, all the people loved them. They remembered them just as they had heard them. They told them to their children. And their children remembered them and told them to other children. By and by men learned to

write. And the great stories God wanted men to know were written down and kept for us."

"Are they in the Bible now? Can I see them? Can you read
them to me?" Bobby asked.

"If you will open the little suitcase and hand me my Bible, I
think I can find one of the old stories to read to you."

So Bobby opened the suitcase and gave his mother the Bible
and she found a place.

"Here is one of the old stories, Bobby," she said. "It is a long
story. I will read you part of it. It is about the great chief, Abram,
who wanted to obey God and to do what was right. He traveled a
long way with all his family and friends into a new country. There
he became very rich. He had many sheep and cattle. His nephew,

whose name was Lot, had many sheep and many cattle, too. The sheep and the cattle had to have water to drink and grass to eat.

"The men who took care of the sheep and the cattle sometimes had a hard time to find enough water and enough grass for all the sheep and all the cattle. So there was a quarrel. I will read how Abram settled the quarrel."

Bobby settled himself comfortably and his mother read him this story from the Bible:

AND Abram was very rich in cattle, and in silver, and in gold.

And Lot also, which went with Abram, had flocks and herds and tents.

And the land was not able to bear them, that they might dwell together. And there was a quarrel between the herdmen of Abram's cattle and the herdmen of Lot's cattle.

And Abram said unto Lot, "Let there be no quarrel between me and thee, and between my herdmen and thy herdmen. Is not the whole land before thee? Separate thyself from me. If thou wilt take the left hand, then I will go to the right; or if thou depart to the right hand, then I will go to the left."

And Lot lifted up his eyes and saw all the plain of the river Jordan, that it was well watered everywhere.

Then Lot chose him all the plain of Jordan; and Lot journeyed east; and they separated themselves the one from the other.

And Abram dwelled in the land of Canaan.

From Genesis 13:2, 5–12

Just as Bobby's mother finished reading about Abram, the train gave a big jerk. Mary woke up and almost rolled off the seat. Her mother caught her quickly.

"That was a big bump, Mary," Bobby said.

Mary looked for a moment as if she were going to cry. Then she smiled instead.

"Big bump," she said. And she sat up and looked out of the window. There were many cows in the fields. She pointed to them. "Cows," she said, "cows." And she laughed and clapped her hands.

Bobby laughed, too. "Many cows," he agreed. "But they seem to have plenty of grass to eat. I hope they don't ever get hungry and thirsty the way Abram's cows did."

Mary did not know what Bobby meant about Abram's cows, but she went on laughing at the cows she saw out of the window.

POEMS ABOUT GOD

BOBBY and his mother and Mary were visiting Grandmother who lived on a farm. One day Bobby and Grandmother and James, the boy next door, were out walking. They were looking for an empty bird nest.

"I know there was a nest in that big bush by the creek back of the barn," Grandmother said. "I saw the birds flying in and out of it this spring."

So Bobby and James and Grandmother went down to the big bush. They looked carefully. And at last they saw a pretty, snug little nest.

"Are you sure the birds are through with it?" Bobby asked.

"Quite sure, Bobby," Grandmother answered. "The little birds have all flown away weeks ago, and the mother bird and the father bird do not need it any more."

"See how smooth it is on the outside," Bobby said. "And all made out of string and little sticks."

"The bird that made that one was a good builder," James agreed. "Not all nests are smooth like that."

He pulled down the branch of the big bush and Bobby saw how well the nest had been tied to the branch.

"That bird knew how to make a safe nest, too," he said. "It wouldn't fall off when the wind blew. And inside it is soft, all lined with feathers."

Bobby looked at his grandmother. "How did the bird learn to make this nest?" he asked.

His grandmother thought a moment. "The wise men who study about birds tell us that the birds do not seem to have to

learn how to make nests, Bobby. When a bird first needs to make a nest, she just seems to know how to make it.''

"But how does she?" Bobby wanted to know. "How does she know without learning?"

"I think we can just say that God planned it that way, dear. God planned for birds to know how to make nests just as he planned for all creatures to have homes."

Bobby and James and Grandmother were all quiet for a moment, looking at the bird nest and thinking about God.

"Once there was a great poet," Grandmother said. "He looked at the wonders in the world, just as we are doing. He thought about God's plan for his world and for caring for all creatures. As he wondered, he talked with God. And God helped him make a poem. The poem has been kept for us in our Bible. It tells about the wonders God has made. I will say part of it for you:

HE SENDETH the springs into the valleys,
They run among the hills.
They give drink to every beast of the field.
By them the birds of the heaven have their habitation,
Which sing among the branches.
He causeth the grass to grow for the cattle,
And herb for the service of man;
That he may bring forth food out of the earth.

The trees of the Lord are full of sap,
Where the birds make their nests.
As for the stork, the fir trees are her house.
The high hills are for the wild goats,
And the rocks are a refuge for the conies.
He appointed the moon for seasons;
The sun knoweth his going down.
O Lord, how manifold are thy works!
In wisdom hast thou made them all.

From Psalm 104

"That poet knew about God's plan," Bobby said. "Is that why his poem was put in the Bible?"

"I think that is the reason, Bobby You see, God wanted us to think of him when we wondered about birds' nests and growing trees and beautiful days and nights. And so he helped the great poet to understand God's plan for his world. He helped him to talk about it in beautiful words which people one day could read."

"Let's go in the house and ask Mother to find that poem in the Bible for us, James," Bobby said. "I want to see where it is written down."

And so they saw the poem in the Bible, as Grandmother had said it was.

RULES FROM LONG AGO FOR NOW

BOBBY and his friend John were on the school playground. It was John's turn to go down the slide. All of a sudden Bobby pushed ahead and ran up the ladder and started down the slide.

"I took your turn! I took your turn!" he called out to John, laughing as if it were a fine joke.

But John did not think it was a good joke. He was angry. He ran up to Bobby as he reached the bottom of the slide. He doubled up his fist to hit Bobby.

"Hey, you fellows," one of the big boys called. "Can't you play without fighting?"

It was Ben. He was in charge of the playground. He came over to the slide.

John stopped. He felt rather silly, with his fist all doubled up and Ben looking at him.

Bobby felt silly, too. "It was my fault," he told Ben. "I took his turn."

"You took his turn?" Ben looked surprised. "I thought you knew that we obeyed the rules on this playground."

"I do know it," Bobby said. "I just thought it would be fun to take John's turn. But it wasn't."

"Well, if you found out that it isn't fun to break the rules, you have learned something important," Ben said. "Give John two turns, and then we will forget it."

John and Bobby looked at each other for a moment. Then they laughed.

"We were acting like babies," John said. "Now watch me do the flying leap! And I am going to take *two* turns just as Ben said I could!"

That night Bobby was talking with his mother.

"I broke the rules at school today," he began. And he told her all about taking John's turn on the slide.

His mother listened. "I am sorry you broke the rules, Bobby," she said. "Rules are for a purpose, you know."

"It isn't fun playing when we break the rules," Bobby agreed. "It makes people mad." He thought awhile.

"Where do rules come from, Mother?" he asked. "Where do we get them?"

"Rules are very, very old, Bobby," his mother told him. "They are like stories and poems. Men learned them before they had learned to write."

"But how did the first rules get made?" Bobby went on.

"You remember, Bobby," his mother began, "that we read from the Bible a big poem about how God planned the world."

"He planned land and water and light and darkness and grass and animals. I remember," Bobby said.

"God planned the world so that we could *depend* upon it," his mother went on. "God made the world so that the sun and the seeds and all things would obey his rules."

"Do the sun and the seeds really obey rules?" Bobby asked.

"Yes, dear. That is how farmers can know when to plant their crops and when to expect them to come up."

Then Bobby remembered about rules for people. "Did God make rules for people, too, Mother?"

"God did make rules for people, son. But there is a great difference about the rules for people," his mother explained. "The sun and the seeds do not choose. They just obey their rules with-out knowing that they are obeying their rules. But with people it is not like that. God lets people decide whether they will obey the rules he made for them or whether they will break the rules. He does not want people to *have* to obey. He wants them to *want* to obey the rules because they love God and trust him."

Bobby thought it over.

"That is better," he decided. "Yes, that is better."

"I think it is, Bobby."

"Did God write his rules in the Bible?" Bobby wanted to know.

"For many, many years God helped the people to learn his rules. Some wise men, called lawgivers, worked with God. They went about the country helping the people to settle their disputes.

OUR RULES

They taught the people God's rules for living. And a long time afterward, the rules came to be in our Bible."

"Where are God's rules in the Bible?" Bobby asked.

"There are several important sets of rules brought together in the Bible for us," his mother explained. "But God's rules are all through the Bible, Bobby. In the stories and poems and laws we find God's rules that help us live happily."

"Read me some of God's rules," Bobby said.

His mother opened the Bible. "Here is one set of rules. It is not long. But it is very important. Jesus said it is the most important of all rules."

THOU shalt love the Lord thy God with all thy heart, and with all thy soul, and with all thy strength, and with all thy mind.	And thou shalt love thy neighbor as thyself. *From* Luke 10:27

Bobby listened as his mother read from the Bible. "Those are big rules," he said.

"They are very big rules, son," his mother agreed. She smiled at Bobby. "But I can think of one way a boy can love his neighbor as himself."

Bobby laughed. "So can I. He can take turns on the slide."

GOD'S PLAN FOR COUNTRIES

BOBBY'S grandmother sent him a present. It was a new book. The book was about America.

There were pictures of mountains and rivers and lakes and the seashore.

There were pictures of big factories and of farms and of forests.

There were pictures of schools and of hospitals and of libraries and of churches.

There were pictures of great men and of great women.

Bobby's daddy read to him in the book about America. It was a good book. It told about the work that the men and women of America did. It told about the ways the other nations of the world had helped America become a great country. It told about the ways America was now helping the other nations of the world.

When his daddy had finished reading, Bobby was feeling very proud of America.

"America is the greatest country in all the world, isn't it, Daddy? It helps other countries more, too."

"Americans think it is the greatest country, Bobby," his daddy answered. "But there isn't just one great country, you know. There are many great countries."

"But America is the *biggest* country, isn't it?"

"Not the biggest country, son, though it is a very big country. But being big doesn't always mean being great. Some of the littlest countries have been very great countries."

"How could they be? What could they do that would be so great?" Bobby wanted to know.

"I will tell you about one country which was very great though it was very small, Bobby. We call it Palestine."

"Tell me how Palestine was a great country," Bobby asked. "Did it help other countries the way America does?"

"It didn't send to the other countries food and clothes and machinery as America does, son. But it gave to many great countries something more important."

"What did it give them?"

"This little country taught the nations about God. The people of Palestine thought about God more than the people of other countries did. They listened to God more."

"Do we have the story of this country?" Bobby asked. "Can you read it to me?"

"The story is in the Bible, son. It is too long a story to read all at once. But there is one part of the story I will read you. It is about a time when the people had forgotten God's rules for them. They had let their church get all dirty and tumble-down.

"Then there came a young king who wanted to do right. He decided to clean up the church and to mend all the broken doors and make it beautiful again. He wanted to obey God, but he did not know God's rules.

"One day when the men were working in the church, they found an old book. They took the book to a man who could read. His name was Shaphan.

"When Shaphan had read the book, he knew that it was a very important book. He knew that it was the book in which the law-givers had written the rules of God for his people. The book had been lost. Now it was found!

"I will read you about this young king who wanted to do right and about what happened when this book was found."

So Bobby's daddy read to him from the Bible:

AND Shaphan told the king saying, "The priest hath delivered me a book."

And Shaphan read it before the king.

When the king had heard the words of the book, he commanded the priest and Shaphan saying, "Go ye, inquire of the Lord for me and for the people concerning the words of this book that is found, because our fathers have not harkened unto the words of this book to do according unto all that which is written concerning us."

And the king went up into the house of the Lord, and all the men with him and all the people both small and great. And he read in their ears all the words of the book which was found in the house of the Lord. And the king stood by a pillar and made a promise before the Lord to keep his commandments. And all the people stood to the promise.

From II Kings 22:10–13; 23:2–3

Bobby took the Bible and put it back on the table.

"Did the people of Palestine remember the rules after that?"

"I wish they had, Bobby. But sometimes they forgot God. Then they did things which were not right."

"Does the Bible tell about that, too?"

"Their great men told the truth about their people. They wrote down how the people disobeyed God's rules for living together. They wrote down how their disobedience to God brought on wars. They wrote down how their disobedience to God caused little children to go hungry. They wrote down how their disobedience to God made people lonely and sad instead of happy and friendly as God intended them to be."

"Is it in the Bible?" Bobby asked.

"It is all in the Bible. And because the story of the little land
of Palestine is in the Bible, people can read it today. They can

learn from it that every country must obey God's rules to have peace and happiness for its people."

"Even great big countries like America?" Bobby wanted to know.

"Even great big countries like America, Bobby."

Bobby picked up his book on America with all the pictures. He looked at it. "I want America to obey God's rules, Daddy," he said.

"So do I, Bobby. Then our great country will be a *good* country. And help all the other countries to be good."

GOD'S PLAN FOR ALL PEOPLES

A NEW family is going to move into our neighborhood," Bobby's mother told him one day. "There is a boy your age and a girl a little younger. And there will be a grandmother to take care of them."

"Goody, I am glad there will be another boy!" Bobby said.

"I think you should know something about the new boy before you meet him, son," his mother said. "These new neighbors are not just like our other neighbors."

"How are they different?" Bobby wanted to know.

"Our new neighbors have come from a very unhappy country, Bobby. They have been very much afraid. Some friends in our country planned for them to come here."

"Then we must be good friends to them," Bobby said. "I will take the boy to school with me and show him where to go."

His mother nodded. "We shall all want to be good friends. They do not know our ways. They do not know our language very well. Their talk will seem strange to us, and our talk will seem strange to them."

The next morning Bobby and little Mary and John and Susan were out in the yard watching the moving wagons bring the furniture to the house where the new neighbors were to live. Bobby's dog Rover was there, too.

A little later they saw a car drive up. A grandmother and a boy about Bobby's size and a girl a little smaller got out.

"They look sick," John said after a moment. "They don't look as if they will be much fun to play with."

Bobby frowned. He thought John was right. But he was remembering what his mother had told him.

"My mother said they have been very unhappy in their own country. They have been afraid. I think we should ask them to come over here and play. I am going to ask them right this minute."

So he went over to the new children. "I am Bobby," he said.

The boy looked at Bobby Then he spoke slowly, as though he did not know the words very well.

"My name is Albert," he said. "My sister's name is Louisa."

Bobby could hardly understand what Albert said.

"Will you come over to my house to play, Albert and Louisa?" was all he could think of to say.

Albert and Louisa nodded solemnly, and so Bobby and the two new children went to his yard.

Bobby told John and Susan the names of the new children and he told Albert and Louisa their names

They all stood looking at one another. Bobby did not know what to do. He wished his mother would come out.

"Do you know how to play fireman?" John asked Albert. The boy shook his head.

"Can you play 'London Bridge Is Falling Down'?" Susan asked Louisa. But the new children only looked puzzled.

"Don't you know any games at all?" John asked.

Just then little Mary, who had been playing by herself, came running up to the other children. She had a flower in each hand. She smiled at the new children.

"Flower," she said. And she gave Albert and Louisa each a flower. Then she laughed. "Run," she called and tagged Albert.

Albert laughed, too. He understood Mary. So he ran, and Mary squealed with delight as he caught the ties on her pinafore and ran after her as if he were driving a horse.

Bobby decided that he would play, too, even though it was a babyish game. He threw Rover's rope around Louisa and called, "Get up, horse, get up!" Louisa ran just as Mary had done. Then John pretended to harness Susan to the wagon, and away they ran. All the children were running and laughing and Rover ran after them barking joyously.

After a while Bobby's mother called to them, "Would the horses and drivers like some lemonade and cookies?"

The children all could understand that, too! So they all sat on the grass and helped themselves.

That evening Bobby was talking with his mother about the new children. "Mary was the only one who knew what to do," he said. "And she is just a baby."

"Well, you see, dear," his mother explained, "Mary doesn't know much of our language, either. And she doesn't know any real games. So the new children were not ashamed to try to play with her."

Bobby was quiet for a moment.

"Are people really different, Mother? I mean, people like Albert and Louisa who live in another country and talk different words? And people like Tito, who looks different from us? And people like Sam, who has different-colored skin?"

"People are different, Bobby. But it isn't their words or eyes or skin that makes the real difference. It is the way they feel inside."

"Then people don't have to be different just because they live in different countries or look different?"

"I think, Bobby, that it is God's plan for people in all nations and people of all colors of skin to understand one another and to like one another and to help one another."

"Does everybody know that, Mother? That it is God's plan?"

"God has been helping people to understand it, Bobby. It takes a long, long time for them to learn."

"Why does it?"

"Long, long ago each family thought that God was their God but not the God of other families. They did not wish to think that God loved all peoples. But the greatest men understood that God wanted all people to know him and work with him and with one another."

"And did the great men help God teach the others?"

"The great men, called the prophets, told the people God's plan for them. They preached to them, and they talked with them by the wayside, and they wrote to them."

"What did the prophets tell the people about God's plan? Do we know what they said?"

"We know some of the words they said, Bobby. They were written down and kept by the people. And after a time they were put in the Bible. We can read them in our Bible today."

"Read me some of the things the prophets said to the people about God's plan for them," Bobby asked.

"I will read you what one of the great prophets said, Bobby.

"He tells them that someday all the people from all countries will pray to God together.

"He tells them that someday all the people from all countries will work together, instead of fighting one another.

"He tells them that someday they will let God decide what is right when they disagree.

"He tells them that someday nobody in any country will be afraid, but that everyone can have his own home and his own garden and orchard.

"This is what this great prophet says:

IT SHALL come to pass, that the house of the Lord shall be established in the top of the mountains. And many nations shall come and say, "Come, and let us go up to the house of God; and he will teach us of his ways, and we will walk in his path."

And he shall judge among many people, and rebuke strong nations afar off.

And they shall beat their swords into plowshares, and their spears into pruning hooks; nation shall not lift up a sword against nation, neither shall they learn war any more.

But they shall sit every man under his vine and under his fig tree; and none shall make them afraid.

For the mouth of the Lord hath spoken it.

From Micah 4:1–4

Bobby sighed. "I wish it was now," he said. "I wish right now that nobody was afraid. I wish right now that everybody would go to church together and do what God planned for them."

"I wish it were right now, too, Bobby. But, you know, God is depending on us, now, to help him. Just as he depended on the great prophets in olden times."

[50]

"How can we help him?" Bobby wanted to know. "We can't write things in the Bible."

"No, but we can help make the things in the Bible come true. And we can let other people know what the Bible says for us to do."

"How can we do that?"

"I think you and Mary and John and Susan made a beginning today, son. You helped Albert and Louisa to forget to be afraid. You helped them to feel that people were friendly and wanted to help them laugh again and be happy. You helped them to feel that having different words and different countries didn't really make people different."

"Is that the way to do it, Mother?" Bobby asked. "Is that the way to make the Bible come true?"

"I think that is the very best way there is to make the Bible come true, Bobby," his mother told him.

WISE SAYINGS OF THE BIBLE

IS THAT a torn place in your sweater, Bobby?" his mother asked one afternoon when Bobby came home from school.

Bobby looked. There in his favorite red-and-white sweater he saw a little hole.

"Now, how did I get that hole in my sweater?"

"However it came, the important thing is to get it mended before it gets any bigger. So off with it, and I'll get my yarn."

"Right this minute?" Bobby asked. "Can't we wait till I take it off tonight?"

"Right this minute, dear," his mother said. "Haven't you heard that old saying, 'A stitch in time saves nine'?"

Bobby pulled his sweater over his head. " 'A stitch in time saves nine,' " he repeated. "If I went out to play with that hole in my sweater, it might get bigger. Then you would have to take more stitches. Is that what the old saying means?"

"That is exactly right, Bobby. So we will take the stitches before you go out to play," his mother said, as she found a piece of yarn the color of the sweater.

"Who thought up that saying, Mother?" Bobby asked. "Where did it come from?"

"I don't know just where that old saying came from, son. We can look it up at the library sometime, if you like. There are many, many old sayings like that. We call them proverbs. People in all countries seem always to have made them up."

"But why did they?" Bobby asked.

"People learn that a certain way of behaving always turns out a certain way," his mother explained, "and so they make up a proverb about it. That proverb reminds them of what they have learned. And it makes an easy way to teach other people, too."

"Do you know any more old proverbs like that one?"

"Oh, many more, Bobby. There is a whole book in the Bible called The Proverbs."

"Is there really, Mother? A whole book of old sayings? Let's look at it." So Bobby brought his mother the Bible, and she found the place and showed him the book called The Proverbs.

"Read me some of the Bible Proverbs," Bobby asked.

"Just let me finish this 'stitch in time' on your sweater, and then I will read some of them to you." So Bobby's mother finished mending the sweater, and Bobby put it on.

"Now read to me," Bobby said.

His mother turned the pages. "There are many of these old sayings in The Proverbs that you would not understand yet, Bobby," she told him. "They were written for grown people. But here are some you may like."

A MERRY HEART
MAKETH
A CHEERFUL
COUNTENANCE

And his mother read to him some wise old sayings from the Bible:

 MERRY heart doeth good like a medicine.

Proverbs 17:22a

A soft answer turneth away wrath;
But grievous words stir up anger.

Proverbs 15:1

A good name is rather to be chosen than great riches,
And loving favor rather than silver and gold.

Proverbs 22:1

Let another man praise thee, and not thine own mouth;
A stranger and not thine own lips.

Proverbs 27:2

The hearing ear, and the seeing eye,
The Lord hath made even both of them.

Proverbs 20:12

A man that hath friends
Must show himself friendly.

Proverbs 18:24a

As his mother finished reading the old saying about having a friend, Bobby heard John calling.

Bobby laughed. "I'd better go play with John, Mother," he said. " 'A man that hath friends

Must show himself friendly!' "

As Bobby ran out of the door, he remembered the sweater. "Thank you, Mother, for taking the 'stitch in time'!" he called.

TELLING ABOUT JESUS

TELL ME about when you were a little boy," Bobby asked his daddy.

His daddy smiled. "Maybe Grandmother or some of her neighbors could tell you better than I could, Bobby."

"Why could they?" Bobby wanted to know.

"Because they know all about when I was a little boy. They remember things I have forgotten."

Just then Mother came into the room. "Grandmother told me a story about something Daddy did, Bobby," she said. "It happened when Daddy was just about your size."

"Tell me all about it," Bobby asked.

"Grandmother had a big loft over the barn. One day Daddy and his brother went up into the loft of the barn to play. They found a broad board. One end of the board was on a block of wood and the other end was on the floor.

" 'Let's jump on the board,' Daddy said to his brother. And he jumped hard on the board. It went up and down. Daddy thought it was a fine jumping board.

"But there was something he had not seen. Some bumblebees had built a nest under the board. When Daddy jumped on the board, it made the nest go up and down, too. This made the bumblebees mad. And the first thing Daddy knew, the bees were buzzing and flying all around him. It seemed as though there were thousands of them."

"Did they sting him?"

"They stung him on the forehead. And Grandmother had to make a poultice and wrap his head up in bandages."

Daddy began to laugh. "I remember that time," he said. "I yelled when I saw those bees, I can tell you! I went down the ladder of the barn quicker than anybody has ever gone down a ladder since!"

Bobby laughed, too. Then he asked his mother, "When I get big, will you remember what I did? Like Grandmother remembers?"

"Daddy and I shall remember many things you did, Bobby. And you will remember some things. And John will remember some things and Susan will remember some things and Henry will remember some things."

Bobby thought of his new book about America. It had some stories in it about great men. He handed it to his daddy.

"Did we get these stories from people who remembered when the men were boys?" Bobby wanted to know.

"That is one important way to get them," his daddy told him. "People who want to write about great men visit the mothers and the teachers and the friends and the neighbors who knew the men. They ask questions. And they find out many things which they put in their books."

Then Bobby's daddy picked up the Bible. "There are stories of great persons in the Bible, too," he said. "There are stories of the greatest person of all the nations."

"That is Jesus," Bobby said.

His daddy nodded.

"Did his mother and his friends tell about him? Is that the way the stories got into the Bible?" Bobby asked.

"I am sure they helped, son," his daddy told him. "The men who wrote the stories of Jesus loved him very much. They wanted to tell others about him. They probably went to the towns where Jesus had lived. They probably talked with his mother and with other people who knew him when he was a boy at home and when he went to school and when he grew up."

"Did they put it all in the Bible for us? Can we read about when Jesus was a boy?"

"They did not put very much in the Bible about when Jesus was a boy, Bobby."

"Why didn't they? I want to know all about what Jesus did when he was a boy."

"I should like to know much more about it, too, son. But the men who wrote the story of Jesus were working with God."

"Didn't God want us to know about when Jesus was a boy?" Bobby asked.

His daddy smiled. 'I do not think it was that way, Bobby. I think the men wrote everything that would show people that Jesus was God's son and man's special helper. What he did when he was a boy was probably just about what other boys did. God planned for him to grow as other boys grew."

"Doesn't the Bible tell us anything about when Jesus was a boy?" Bobby asked.

"There are a few stories about when Jesus was a baby," his daddy said. "And there is one story about when Jesus was a boy."

"Read me that one."

"It is a story about a trip Jesus made with Mary and Joseph and a group of their friends. They went from their home town of Nazareth to the big city of Jerusalem. They went to the church which they called the temple. Then Jesus' parents and friends started home. But Jesus stayed in Jerusalem. Mary and Joseph thought he was lost. And then they found him. This is the story:

Now HIS parents went to Jerusalem every year at the feast of the passover.

And when Jesus was twelve years old, they went up to Jerusalem.

And as they returned, the child Jesus stayed behind in Jerusalem; and Joseph and his mother knew not of it. But they, supposing him to have been in the company, went a day's journey; and they sought him among their kinsfolk and friends.

And when they found him not, they turned back again to Jerusalem, seeking him.

And they found him in the temple, sitting with the teachers both hearing them and asking them questions.

And he went down with them, and came to Nazareth, and obeyed them.

And Jesus grew in wisdom and stature, and in favor with God and man.

From Luke 2:41–46, 51, 52

STORIES JESUS TOLD

BOBBY thought Rover was lost. He had been away from home all afternoon. Bobby and John were looking for him.

They walked down one street and up another street and then down another street. They were a long way from home. They did not know the boys and girls on that street.

Just then they saw Rover. A boy was petting him.

Bobby ran toward the dog. Rover wagged his tail and tried to get up. Then Bobby saw that Rover's leg was all bandaged up.

"How did he get hurt?" Bobby asked the boy.

And the boy told him that Rover had been hit by a ball when he ran out on a field where the boys were playing baseball.

"Did you take care of him? Did you fix his leg?" John asked.

"I brought him home and my mother helped me fix it. We washed it and put some medicine on it and wrapped it up. I think it feels better."

"I am glad you were there when Rover got hurt," Bobby told the boy. "You were good to him."

"He is a fine dog. I like him," the boy answered.

"I think we will take him home now," Bobby said. "We have a long way to go."

Then Bobby and John looked at each other.

They wondered how they could carry Rover. They knew he should not walk so far on his hurt leg.

"Would you like to borrow my wagon?" the boy asked. "Rover could ride in the wagon. You could bring it back tomorrow."

"Would you lend it to us?" Bobby said. "That will be a good way to get him home."

And so Bobby and John put Rover into the boy's wagon and started home.

"We will be sure to bring it back to you tomorrow," Bobby told the boy.

As soon as they were home, Bobby fed Rover. Then Daddy looked at the leg and said it would soon be well.

"That boy was nice to take care of Rover," Bobby said. "He didn't know us, either. He wasn't a friend or a neighbor or anything."

"Maybe he was a neighbor, Bobby," Daddy said.

"How could he be, Daddy? He lives on another street. We don't even know his name. How could he be our neighbor?"

"Once a man asked Jesus a question. He asked 'Who is my neighbor?' And Jesus taught a new meaning of neighbor."

"How did Jesus teach a new meaning of a word?" Bobby wanted to know.

"He told them a story to show them the new meaning," his daddy said. "Because it is important for us to know the new meaning Jesus taught, the story has been kept for us in the Bible."

"Read me the story Jesus told," Bobby asked. "Read it to me from the Bible."

So his daddy found the story in the Bible and read it:

AND Jesus said:
"A certain man went down from Jerusalem to Jericho and fell among thieves, which stripped him of his clothes and wounded him, and went away, leaving him half dead.

"But a certain Samaritan, as he journeyed, came where he was; and when he saw him, he had compassion on him and went to him and bound up his wounds, pouring in oil and wine, and set him on his own beast, and brought him to an inn, and took care of him.

"And on the morrow when he left, he took out two pieces of money and gave them to the host, and said unto him, 'Take care of him; and whatsoever thou spendest more, when I come again, I will repay thee.' "

(Jesus finished the story Then he looked at the man who had asked him, "Who is my neighbor?")

"Which now of these, thinkest thou, was neighbor unto him that fell among the thieves?"

And he said, "He that showed mercy on him."

Then said Jesus unto him, "Go, and do thou likewise."

From Luke 10:30, 33–37

Bobby listened to the story.

"To tell a story is a good way to show people what it means to be a neighbor," he said.

"Jesus told many stories to help people understand what he taught them," his daddy told him.

Bobby was pleased. He liked to think of Jesus telling stories.

"Are there lots of Jesus' stories in the Bible?" he asked.

"There are a good many, son. We call them parables. The one I read you is the favorite parable of many persons."

"It is a good story," Bobby agreed. "I like what it says about neighbor. Being a neighbor is to help people." He thought a moment.

"Then that boy who helped Rover *is* my neighbor? Even if I don't know his name?" he asked.

"The hurt man in the story Jesus told did not know the Samaritan's name," his daddy reminded him. "He just knew that somebody had taken care of him."

"But I think I will find out my neighbor's name when I take his wagon back tomorrow," Bobby said.

LETTER WRITERS OF THE BIBLE

BOBBY heard the postman's whistle.

"Maybe there is a letter from Grandmother," he called to his mother and ran to the door. Sure enough, there was a letter from Grandmother.

"Do we have to wait until Daddy comes home to read it?"

Mother looked at the envelope. "It has *all* our names on it; so I think Daddy would like us to open it."

"Then let's read it right now," Bobby said.

"Let's dress Mary first, shall we, Bobby? She is through her nap now, and she will not like to wait while we read the letter. It looks like a nice, long letter."

Bobby held the letter in his hand. "I wonder if Grandmother will tell us about the baby puppies," he said. "They were such pretty puppies."

"I think she will tell us about them."

"And will she tell us about James?"

"Grandmother usually remembers to tell us all the news, doesn't she, son? That is why we always like her letters so much."

Mary was ready for her dress.

"Now, Mary, if you will listen to Grandmother's letter, you will hear about the puppies," Bobby said.

And so Bobby's mother opened the envelope and read the letter. Sure enough, Grandmother told about the puppies and about James and about the garden and about the chickens, and all the other things that Bobby wanted to know.

"Read it again," he said. "I want to hear it again."

So his mother read it again.

"I like to get letters," Bobby said.

"Almost everybody likes to get letters," his mother told him. "They help us to feel near to people."

"Yes, they do. I can just hear Grandmother talking when you read me her letter."

"Letters are often very important," his mother went on.

"Tell me about some important letters," Bobby asked.

"There are some letters in the Bible, Bobby."

Bobby was surprised. "How did letters get in the Bible, Mother? Did God write them?"

"Not as Grandmother wrote this letter. But God helped the men who wrote them. God helped the men to know what to say in the letters."

"But who wrote them?"

"Some of them were written by a man whose name was Paul. He was a teacher. He went from city to city teaching the people about God. He told them about Jesus. Then, when he left one city to go to another, he would write the people a letter."

"Were they good letters? Like Grandmother's?" Bobby asked.

"The people who received the letters thought they were very good letters, Bobby."

"What did they tell about?"

"They talked about friends. They talked about what Paul had been doing since he left them. But most of all they talked about God and about Jesus and about how people should live."

"Let's read one of Paul's letters," Bobby said.

"Paul's letters were written to grown people, Bobby. I do not think you would understand them yet."

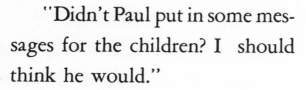

"Didn't Paul put in some messages for the children? I should think he would."

His mother thought awhile. "Sometimes he did, I think," she said. She opened the Bible. "Here is a letter Paul wrote to the people in the church at a city named Ephesus."

"What does it say?"

"I will read part of it to you, Bobby. I will read you the beginning of the letter, and then I will read a part of what Paul wrote to the grown people, and then I will read the message he sent to the children."

PAUL, an apostle of Jesus Christ by the will of God, to the church members at Ephesus:

Let all bitterness and anger and evil-speaking be put away from you;

And be ye kind one to another, tender-hearted, forgiving one another, even as God for Christ's sake hath forgiven you.

Children, obey your parents in the Lord: for this is right.

Honor thy father and mother; that it may be well with thee.

From Ephesians 1:1; 4:31, 32; 6:1–3

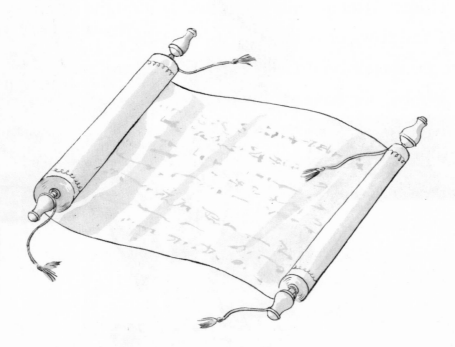

THE BIBLE LIBRARY

BOBBY was in the children's room at the library. He was looking at some pictures. After a while he walked around the room looking at the rows and rows of books.

"There are lots of books in this room," he said to the librarian.

"Yes, Bobby, we have many books for children. And in another room there are many more books for grown people."

"May I take a book home for my mother to read to me?"

And so the librarian wrote Bobby's name on a card and Bobby took the book home.

"I went to the library," he told his mother. "I brought a book for you to read to me."

"Good, Bobby!"

"I am glad we have a library. I like books."

"All the persons in our family like books," his mother said. "Grandmother and Daddy and Mother and Bobby. Even little Mary likes picture books."

"You told me about the time before there were any books. People must have missed them."

"I think people learned to make books because they needed them, Bobby."

"Is that why people made the Bible? Because they needed it?"

"That is why we have the Bible, dear. Because people need it. God knew that people needed it. And so he planned for the wise men and the good men to help him make it."

"The Bible is a big book," Bobby said.

"Do you know that the Bible is really a library?" his mother asked.

Bobby looked surprised. "How can it be a library, Mother? A library is many books."

"And the Bible is many books, Bobby. It isn't just one book. All the books are put together, but there are many separate books."

Bobby did not understand about it.

"Many different writers helped to write the books in the Bible library," his mother explained.

"Show me," Bobby asked.

And so his mother showed him. She opened the Bible. "You see, here is a book called Genesis. This is the book that has the great poem in it about the beginning of the world. It is one of the finest storybooks in the Bible, too. The story about Abraham and his nephew is in this book."

Then she found another page.

"This book is called Psalms. This is the book of beautiful poems and hymns. We have read some of them." Bobby nodded his head. He remembered some of the poems.

"And then way over here are four other books," his mother went on. "They are called Matthew and Mark and Luke and John. They were given the names of the men who people thought helped write them. They are four books of stories about Jesus."

Bobby took the Bible in his own hands. "Then I have a whole library in my hands," he said.

"That's right, Bobby. You have a whole library in your hands."

"But I think it should be bigger," Bobby said. "I should think it would be the biggest library in all the world."

His mother laughed. "Bobby, how you do like things to be big!" she said. "You are always asking Daddy and me if something is the biggest in the world!"

Bobby laughed, too. Then he was quiet. "But the Bible should be big. It is God's special book."

"But you know, dear, that the biggest things aren't always the most important to God. Little babies are about the most important creatures on earth to God."

Bobby thought it over. "That's right," he said. "I guess things don't have to be big to be important."

He thought some more. "And it is a good thing the Bible library isn't the biggest in the world. Because then it would be too big for people to have in their houses. And they need it in their houses."

THE BIBLE FOR EVERY DAY

TOM was a boy who went to Bobby's school. But he did not learn so fast as the others did.

One day the boys and girls were playing a game. It was a game that had counting in it. It was Tom's turn to count. He got all mixed up.

Instead of saying, "One, two, three, four, five," as the other boys and girls did, Tom would say, "One, three, five, four."

The other boys and girls laughed at him. Then they told him he could not play any more because he did not know how to count. And Tom sat by himself and looked unhappy.

When Bobby came home from school that day, he sat on his front porch and thought. He thought about Tom.

Bobby looked up and saw his daddy coming home. He ran to meet him.

"It isn't right to laugh at people, is it, Daddy?" he asked.

"Sometimes it is right, son. It is right when people are having fun with one another. When all the people are having fun."

"Tom wasn't having fun today," Bobby said. And he told his daddy about the way the other boys and girls had laughed at Tom because he could not count in the game.

"That was not a good time to laugh, Bobby. That was making someone unhappy."

"What should I do when they laugh at him?" Bobby wanted to know.

"What do you think about it, son?"

Bobby thought awhile. "I might help him. I might say, 'I will count with you, Tom.'"

"I think that would be good, son. That would help Tom keep the numbers straight."

"Or I might say that we could play another game that did not have counting in it."

"That might be good, too," Daddy agreed. Then he went on, "There is a verse in the Bible that I think might help you know when to laugh and when not to laugh. It says, 'Be ye kind one to another.' Sometimes it isn't kind to laugh."

"I have heard that verse," Bobby said. "Mother read it to me right out of the Bible."

"I like to have Bible verses in my mind, Bobby," Daddy said. "They often help me to know what to do."

"Do they, Daddy?"

"I remembered one this very morning, son."

"How did it help you?"

"Something happened that made me angry. I wanted to say something ugly to a man. Then I remembered that old saying from the wise men,

> 'A soft answer turneth away wrath;
> But grievous words stir up anger. "

Bobby nodded. "I have heard that one, too. It is a good saying."

Daddy went on. "That old saying reminded me that if I say something ugly I will just 'stir up anger' in the other person. And so I decided to try a 'soft answer' instead of saying something ugly. And it worked!"

"Is that the way the Bible helps us? By telling us what to do?"

"That is one way it helps us, Bobby."

"Then it is good to have the Bible in our minds. I think I will learn some of the Bible," Bobby decided. "I will learn the part about being kind. Say it to me again, Daddy."

" 'Be ye kind one to another.' "

" 'Be ye kind one to another,' " Bobby repeated. "I will remember that."